T0117044

Pride, Abuse, & Mental Illness

A series of Short Stories

By
Ms. Paulajean Anne Anderson
& collaborated with
John F. Morales

authorHOUSE®

AuthorHouse™
1663 Liberty Drive
Bloomington, IN 47403
www.authorhouse.com
Phone: 1-800-839-8640

First published by AuthorHouse 3/7/2011

ISBN: 978-1-4567-3918-8 (e)
ISBN: 978-1-4567-3919-5 (dj)
ISBN: 978-1-4567-3920-1 (sc)

Library of Congress Control Number: 2011902166

Printed in the United States of America

Book Dedication

To my mom who has experienced over fifty-six years of abuse. This abuse completely stopped when my dad passed away August 18, 2009. I also would like to dedicate this book to those who have experienced abuse and are afraid to speak up about it.

By: PJ (Author 2009)

Disclaimer

The names mentioned in this book have been changed so that there will be no hard feelings. Similarities to actual events may be incidental even though some of the stories discussed may be true.

By: PJ (Author 2009)

Part 1

A World of Abuse
By: PJ (Author 2009)

A Meeting of Chance

Mary was twenty-one years old when she served in the Civil Air Patrol located in Orlando, Florida. She was very good at doing clerical, filing, and office work. Her biggest asset was that she could type more than 120 words per minute and had an excellent memory for minute details.

Mary graduated at the top of her class in high school. Prior to going into the service, she attended college but only completed one year and was shy of completing her Associates degree. She felt that becoming part if the Civil Air Patrol was her way of fighting for a cause that she believed in.

Mary was a victim of an estranged dysfunctional family. She can remember the abuse she saw her mom go through the hands of her natural father. She had even witnessed her mom commit suicide with a gun. When her mom was dead she ended up being adopted out with her other siblings.

During this time period the Korean War was going on. There were many people who felt that participating in the military was a great cause and a way to serve the United States. This was especially true with those that believed democracy for all. Mary was one of these individuals.

It was New Years Eve 1952. Mary decided since she had a break from her Civil Air Patrol camp, to attend a USO dance with one of her friends. While at the dance she and her friend met a couple of Marines. Toward the end of the dance Mary found herself attracted to a Sergeant by the name of Frank.

Frank had been a cook in the Marines for over 2-years. He had a month of leave before reporting to his new assignment in Okinawa, Japan. He was a great dancer and was also attracted to Mary. They spent the whole night dancing together. When the stroke of midnight occurred they ended up in each other's arms and kissed. After the dance was over Frank walked Mary back to her room on base. Since it was the weekend, they met up a couple more times. Finally they consummated their relationship by the third date and they were in love.

After about a week in Florida Frank decided that he wanted to go to Milwaukee, Wisconsin to visit his folks before he shipped out. He invited Mary and she accepted without hesitation. Their flight to Milwaukee took about 6-hours. While on the airplane Frank and Mary did a lot of talking. Through their conversations they discovered that they might truly be soul mates. They arrived in Milwaukee, Wisconsin on January 10, 1953. From the airport they took a taxicab to his folks.

Meet a Dysfunctional Abusive Family

Frank and Mary arrived at his parent's home by mid-afternoon. Mary was excited because she was meeting the parents of the man she fell in love with for the first time. Frank also was so excited that he was tongue tied and said very little.

Initially Mary and Jodi got along famously. They even left Frank and his dad Jack in the kitchen and went to the front of the house. Jodi wanted to know everything about May and just have some girl talk away from the guys.

While the girls were away Jack and Frank talked. They did so while drinking beer and whiskey. They also talked in Polish and English.

After a few drinks Frank finally opened up. He told Jack about his relationship with Mary. He let him know that he was in love and planned to marry her if everything worked out right. Frank also shared that he was going to Okinawa, Japan and he wanted his dad Jack to watch after Mary while he was away. Jack agreed to do so and welcomed Mary as part of their family.

Later that evening Jodi and Mary prepared a quick dinner of goulash with a salad and butter biscuits. After dinner they also enjoyed some apple pie with a side of ice cream. Frank and Jack then continued to drink their beer and whiskey and Mary joined them.

During the next few weeks Frank and Mary spent as much time as possible together. They worked together to get Mary settled in and to prepare for Frank's assignment in Okinawa. During the last couple of days of Frank's leave Mary made sure that he made it to his ship on time for his deployment.

Once Frank was on his way to Okinawa, Mary worked on finishing up her term with the Civil Air Patrol. She only had a couple more months to complete before receiving her discharge. About 3-months after Frank had been gone Mary found out that she was 8-weeks pregnant. She knew that this was Frank's baby because she had not been with anyone else.

Shortly after Frank found out about this news, he did not believe it. Instead he thought Mary was sleeping around while he was away. Jodi added to these rumors in her letters to her son. Jack stayed out of it because he wanted to keep the promise he made to Frank.

Once Mary was out of the military she asked if she could stay with Jack and Jodi until she had her baby. Of course Jack said yes, but Jodi was dead against it. She felt that Mary was trying to trick her middle son into marriage. Of course this definitely was not the case.

As soon as Mary moved in there were many problems. Jodi and her clashed. They were always fighting or bickering over something. Jack just stayed to himself, but would step in when these arguments got out of control.

By the end of June 1953, Frank came home for a short leave. During that time he and Mary got married. Once married he started sending money to Jack for Mary's room and board. He also made sure that Mary had enough money to care for herself.

Of course the little money that Mary received was not enough. This why she chose to obtain a part time job with the Milwaukee Credit Bureau. She would be working as a collections agent and as a clerk. This is when her experience in the Civil Air Patrol paid off. She was able to save enough money to move when Frank was discharged from the Marines. On December 18, 1953 Mary had a bouncing baby boy. The name chosen was Paul and he was severely underweight.

By April 1954 Frank finally received his Honorable Discharge from the Marine Corps. The only position he was trained to do was a baker, but these positions were hard to find. This is why he took a position at a West Allis, Wisconsin foundry.

Around June 1954 Mary, Frank, and Paul moved into their first house on Greenfield Boulevard. Frank continued to work at the foundry but he didn't like to come home after work. Instead he would hang out with his friends at a local bar.

While at this bar Frank would drink a lot, play pool, and flirt with the ladies. Most of the time Mary had to find him and bring him home. When this happened there always was a lot of screaming, arguing, and physical abuse.

Later in this year Mary found out that she was pregnant again. She was going to have another boy. When Frank found out about the pregnancy he was more accepting. He stopped the physical abuse but continued to verbally, psychologically, and emotionally abuse Mary. Sometimes this abuse was so bad that Mary had to leave and take long walks. Finally on July 5, 1955 Tim was born.

Tim was an average sized baby boy. When he was born he had

Rheumatic Fever, went into convulsions, and almost died. He did survive though after a lot of hospitalizations and medications.

Shortly after Tim was born the family needed a larger place to live. This is when they found a large two-story house on 32nd Street. This house was close to Frank's parents and to several Catholic churches.

Frank and Mary did not trust the public school system so the decided to send all of their children to a private Catholic school. This meant that Frank had to work harder to support his family. He chose to work at least two jobs so he was hardly ever home.

A year after moving into this new home Mary was pregnant again. This time she was going to have her first girl.

During this pregnancy Frank was nicer to Mary because he did want the girl as much as Mary did. He even cut back on his drinking, but he still drank a lot. Knowing that he had another child on the way Frank worked harder than usual. He left the foundry and started working for the American Motor Corporation as a laborer and assembler. He also started to do carpenter work and painting jobs on the weekends.

April was born on June 16, 1957. She was very healthy and was one of the largest children that Mary had. Frank was very proud of his new baby girl and loved to show her off when he had a chance.

Shortly after April was born Frank and Mary planned a trip to Florida. Mary wanted to see her sister, brother, and stepfather. She also thought that by making the trip some of the abuse she was receiving from Frank would stop. This trip was scheduled for the summer of 1958.

By September 1959 Mike was born. Shortly after his birth the family moved into a larger house that had a yard. This new house needed a lot of work. Frank and decided that they would the work themselves. They figured that by doing the work themselves that they could save money.

This new home was located on Becher Street. It was located in a culley-sack away from most of the busy streets. This location was ideal for raising a family. There also was a huge yard that required a lot of work to maintain.

With this move Frank and Mary continued to have huge fights. Frank work put his fists through walls and doors all of the time. Mary would end up in tears or bruises all over her body. She would leave for her long walks say, "I'm going to leave him this time." When Mary left Paul would chase after her. Paul would try to convince Mary to come back home for the sake of the family. As Paul caught up with Mary, he would find out other things that were happening.

Shortly after Mary left Frank he would freak out. He did not want to raise all of these children alone. He felt that the task would drive him crazy. This is when he would promise Mary that he would completely stop the abuse. Mary would believe him and returned home for the sake of the family. The abuse never truly stopped.

Rick was born in October 1960. Again he was a healthy boy. Now with five children Mary was kept busy. Frank was never home except to pay bills. He and Mary would put the older children to work. The money they made would go toward the household with a promise that it would be paid back.

Frank continued to abuse Mary physically, verbally, psychologically, and emotionally. When he was done with abusing

Mary he would do the same with his older children especially Paul the eldest. Paul would fight back and Frank threatened to kill him if he did so again. From that point on Paul no longer had any respect for his dad Frank.

During the next 2-years Nick and Loni were born. Since Paul was the eldest of the seven children he had the responsibility of caring for his siblings. He did so most of the time for free. He also verbally and physically abusive toward the younger boys. As he continued to get older his responsibility increased. He also started to drink like his mom and dad. Besides drinking he became involved in doing drugs, stealing, and was always in fights.

Tim followed a similar pattern to Paul his older brother. The difference is he would start to talk back to Frank and Mary. He loved to be the center of attention especially when he was right. This type of rebellion ended up getting him into trouble most of the time.

In early 1972 Paul entered the United States Army. He felt that this would be a way from getting away from the violence and abuse in the household. Paul didn't know that the problems he left were worse than he witnessed. He also didn't know that Tim gave up on the family in his own ways. This is why when Paul entered into the military Tim was placed into a detention home.

As a Family Changed

On February 28, 1972 Paul entered the service. He was not the first sibling to leave this family. Tim was the first to leave because he became unmanageable and was out of control. Frank could now handle him without wanting to kill him. Tim was placed in a detention home at least until he turned 18 years old.

When Paul went into the army he still was an alcoholic and a drug addict. He mainly went in to get away from violence and abuse he saw and received at home. What he found is that the anger he kept inside was enhanced. He also went back to his past drug scene and became even more addicted. This is why for the first 9-months in the army he was not promoted. Paul also had a culture shock because he never had been around guns before. By the end of 1972 Paul met someone for the first time. Sheila lived in a board-and-care home for unruly adolescents. She was there due to her history of prostitution and drugs. Sheila was even unmanageable.

When Paul met Sheila he thought that he was in love. He just wanted to be around her all of the time. He didn't even care about her situation or circumstances. In fact, he would leave early on the weekends just to be with her. He thought he was going to be her knight in shining armor.

Due to the drugs and alcohol Paul was very confused. He

had no control on his impulsiveness and emotions. He also was naive to relationships due to his true lack of experience. By his nineteenth he was able to get Sheila released into his custody. This is when they started living together.

In March 1973 Sheila and Paul married. Sheila's dad gave her away and helped them out their first night and month. Everyone in the apartment complex helped them get started and partied with them all night long.

Shortly after getting married Paul got into trouble. He crashed a military vehicle and made some poor decisions. Paul lost his new rank and pay. he had been restricted to the base for several weeks. Being a rebel Paul kept breaking this restriction. He just wanted to be with Sheila as much as he could.

After getting married Paul found out that Sheila was pregnant. He also found out that he was going to receive another class in Texas. This is when he decided to take Sheila with him.

While taking the class Sheila was having a lot of problems with her pregnancy. She was very dehydrated, not eating enough, and having other complications. These problems contributed to the stress that Paul was already having with his courses. He ended up failing the course and had to return to Colorado. Prior to returning he sent Sheila home to be with her mom and to have the baby. When the baby was born Paula was high on drugs.

That same year Paul was shipped to Kansas. While in Kansas he continued to party and still did not get promoted. Sheila threatened Paul about not ever seeing Tori if he didn't quit the drugs and alcohol. Paul took this threat to heart and decided to enter into rehabilitation. He ended up getting clean of all drugs and alcohol in under 3-months. Once he was completely clean he started to regain his ranks back.

In November 1973 Sheila and Tori joined Paul in Kansas. A week later Paul ended up going to Germany for an exercise. While he was in Germany Tori was taken away from Sheila. The reason was because of child abuse. This situation caused Paul to return early from the exercise. By mid-December Tori was returned to Paul and Sheila. They were placed on probation for about 9-months.

After his return from Germany Paul obtained two more promotions. Everything was not wine and roses though with his marriage to Sheila. They would have knock down and dragged out fights. These were verbally and physically usually with Sheila getting the brunt end of it. Sheila would go back to her old games of prostitution, alcohol, and drugs and would lie about while Paul took care of Tori. Due to the abuse Sheila received she still continued to abuse and neglect Tori. Paul could see why Tori were taken away in the first place.

In 1974 Paul was transferred back to Colorado. He was doing very well since he was off of the drugs. Even though he was doing well, Sheila was interfering with his career. She continued the same behavior she had in Kansas. By doing so Paul was under unwanted stress.

In mid-1975 Paul was scheduled to go be stationed in Germany. He knew that his family could not go with him initially so he sent them back to California. He accepted that Sheila and him were not going to last in their marriage. This is why he chose to give Sheila the ultimatum of not coming to join him in Germany.

Paul had been in Germany for 6-months and he sent for his

family. When they joined him nothing truly had changed in the relationship. Sheila was still sleeping around, drinking, and doing drugs. Tori was even being neglected and abused. Finally after about 9-months of these behaviors Paul had enough. He took Sheila and just about killed her with his bare hands in front of witnesses.

When this happened he was locked up. About a month later he was able to get Tori out of the picture and back to the United States. From that point on Paul decided to get out of the military and try to raise his daughter. In June 1976 he did receive his discharge.

Once out of the military Paul lived with his parents for a month. He found that living at home was not going to work for him because the abuse he left when he was 18-years old was still there. He knew as an adult he did not need to be around it especially since he started to show these behaviors in Germany when he almost killed Sheila with his bare hands.

Paul moved into an efficiency apartment with Tori. He tried to raise Tori on his own but found that he was too immature to do so. He could not work or have a relationship with Tori there. This is why he let his parents know what was going on. When this happened Frank and Mary started to raise Tori on a temporary basis which only lasted about 6-months.

When Paul received Tori back he found that he was becoming neglectful and abusive to Tori. Tori were even temporarily taken away from him for leaving Tori in an automobile during the middle of winter.

Paul was able to get Tori back, but he was not really ready to raise her. His abuse got worse. Due to his guilt and the fear that he would kill Tori, Paul placed Tori with the state. He then left Wisconsin and ended up in California.

While in California Paul met Kate. Kate was about 6-years older than Paul. The difference is she was very immature for her age but Paul didn't care.

Six months into the relationship Paul brought Kate back to Wisconsin with him. He had to be there to make his divorce final with Sheila. During that time he also visited with his daughter through a monitored visit. Several months later Tori were placed with Frank and Mary permanently.

Repeated Multiple Abuse

Initially when Paul and Kate started their relationship they got along very well. After only a couple of months living together all of that changed. This was especially true because Paul went back to his drinking and drugs.

Paul and Kate would fight every day. First the fights would start out verbally. From there they would end up psychological, emotional, and physical, with both being sure that they got their licks in. Eventually Kate would get the worst end of the abuse even though she started these fights. These fights continued on during their stay in Wisconsin. About 8-months later they moved back to California.

While in California Kate continued to be abused by Paul. This happened until her dad Pete stepped in and threatened Paul.

Paul did take this threat seriously. He sought out psychological help and was started on medication. When this happened most of the abusive behaviors stopped. He still had verbal arguments with Kate, but no he was no longer physical toward her. When he stopped being physical so did Kate. The only thing is these behaviors were only short lived.

Kate would start up all over again with her abuse. Instead of dealing with these problems Paul would just take it and keep everything inside. After 7 ½ years Paul left this relationship. He felt if he didn't that he would kill Kate or be killed. He also started a new relationship with a co-worker.

More Abuse Trouble

Paul met Shelly while on the job. He found that he was competitive and Shelly was willing to give him competition. Shelly was his same age and a mother of three children. She was having problem in her present marriage with abuse and neglect. She felt that her husband was not paying enough attention to her and was using her. The truth is the situation was just the opposite, as you will see here.

Shelly and Paul got along very well initially. They were always together and even took unnecessary risks while on the job. Eventually Paul had to leave because he knew that it would be better for Shelly.

Paul found an efficiency apartment on his own. Several months later Shelly moved in. At first this was without her children. Around 6-8 months later the children moved in and they had to find a larger place to live.

Since Paul was a veteran they bought a house while using a veterans housing loan. Because it was California the only type of home that they could afford was a 3-bedroom townhouse. They lived in Santa Ana, California for 11-years. During that time Paul received verbal abuse most of the time. He also was almost never home because he worked multiple jobs including being in the military.

Toward the end of the relationship he found out that he was being used to help raise and support Shelly's children. When he realized this it angered him and this relationship ended by becoming an emotional, psychological, verbal, and physically abusive one. There was more hurt this time because he thought that this relationship would work.

Still Being Used

When Paul's last relationship ended he was very traumatized. He decided that he didn't care any more so he decided to look elsewhere for relationships. He became gay thinking that this might be the answer. Of course moving in this direction was not any better. Paul still was belittled, put down, and used. The only thing that kept him going is he was still capable of holding down a job even after getting injured.

Paul would wear his heart on his sleeve. He would try to help those less fortunate than him either financially or morally. He also did go back to using his drugs and alcohol again. The path he was headed in was backwards. There was no one to blame but himself. The reason is because he allowed others to take advantage of him.

While living a gay life style Paul was discriminated against. He was accused of things that he never did. These accusations happened not only once but several times in different environments.

Thinking about what Paul had been through over 30-years one would think that he would have learned to care for himself. He didn't though initially because his daughter Tori used him especially when his guard was down. This was mostly psychologically and financially and was done with no remorse.

Paul is still vulnerable to being used. He is stronger, but still has a heart of gold that can be broken at the drop of a hat. He is angered because everything that had happened to him could have been prevented had he been brought up with the nurturing of a loving father and mother.

Lessons Learned

As Paul found out throughout his experiences in relationships the only way that they will work is if each participant works together and respect one-another. If they don't the relationship will not work and end up in some form of abuse causing hurt, hard feelings, emotional and psychological trauma. There will be no winner.

When Paul tried to help his mom Mary when she was receiving abuse from Frank, the help or assistance was not accepted willingly. Instead Mary chose to deny that there was a problem. The reason for doing so is because she had become co-dependent and accustomed to the abuse even though it would tear her up inside.

Facing Our Mortality

Today so many of us either have not faced, or take our mortality for granted. In this story Paul was no different. In fact, he believed that his took own mortality completely and totally for granted. He thought that he was invincible which is the mistake many of us make until we really take a good hard look at our true self and decide to make changes.

Paul had been married for almost all of his life as an adult. During these marriages he tried to be the Spiritual head of his household. This was a task that never had been trained for because he had no example to dwell on since he had an abusive father and mother in Frank and Mary. His my anger and other barriers made him weak and vulnerable. This is the reason that the marriages did not last. It is also the reason so many experience a lot of hurt during the divorce process.

The hurt seen was not only to him; it involved an innocent 5-year old girl, a 9-year-old boy and others. Even today healing is happening but this is not an ending process. Know where the healing is with the others is very involved. The main reason is due to lack of communication.

Hurt could have been avoided Paul truly been able to experience love from his immediate family. Paul was lost and had no direction mainly because the behaviors he demonstrated in his relationships were learned from abusive parents.

Today as part of hindsight I believe the answer that Paul was looking for can only be found through prayer, counseling, communication, and love. So what happened?

As the situation with Paul, the night I found out I no longer was going to have a marriage I panicked. I felt that my life had just fallen and taken from beneath me and I could do nothing to salvage it. I was ready to end it all at my own hand with a knife because of the emotional and psychological hurt that I experienced. This is when I started to pray. Something inside me told me that through prayer there is an answer. God will help you and take care of you. He has not given up on you.

I prayed all night long and God spared me this wrongful death. God had me face me for who I was and what I was about to do for once. He had me face my problems and yes, my morality. The difference this time is I tried to listen but did not understand. My revelation of this evening did not stop the divorce. In fact, everything turned out with my significant other and I hating each other in the end.

As Paul I felt used, abused, and taken advantage of. I also was very angry because I was working at being a better parent and provider and was not successful. I even cut my hours to be there more for my family. The problem was it was to late.

My significant other had already been involved with someone else for 3 months before I had a chance to make a difference. This was done on the sly without me knowing even though I suspected that there was a problem with something different in the relationship.

In a matter of 2 months I ended up having a major nervous breakdown twice. Once in front of my significant other, the other on Christmas Eve. I was treated for both of these with different types of medication, which took off the edge, but my problems, was not resolved completely.

Due to my emotional instability I had lost my regular job so I started working with a nursing registry. The year was 1997. As 1998 came around I found another full time job in an acute hospital. I was out of practice with my nursing skills and made a lot of mistakes. I still was not very stable emotionally, which did not help matters.

This job only lasted me 3 months. I quit after being accused of killing a 96-year-old female who was dying when I received her. At this point I was not even sure about who I was anymore. I took another look at myself and found that I had not faced my true self yet. A self I had kept hidden due to denial for well over 33 years. I decided to follow the direction I am living today whether it is right or wrong.

While living this new life I have maintained and hung on to a reality and not a fantasy perspective. I also believe God has been guiding and watching over me even though I have been a terrible sinner and a harlot. He has forgiven me.

There also had been one more nervous breakdown. It happened in September 1998. I was ready to take my life again. This time though, it was a test to see if I really have any friends including my parents. God did provide me that answer after having me face my morality and mortality. Today God is my best friend. He knows all that I have done and what I am to do. He is my Savior. He will never leave me nor forsake me.

In June of 2001 I was headed to Thailand for Gender Reassignment Surgery. Making this trip was very terrifying especially with me flying and being in another country alone. The surgery I underwent could kill me if I would bleed out or have respiratory complications secondary to my smoking history. Again I had to face my own mortality to go through with everything. Through prayer everything went very well. Even today I still have not had any major complications.

As we all will never forget September 11, 2001. Many of the police and fire officers faced their mortality when they went in to try to rescue others. A lot of them died in the process. The episode of loosing the Twin Towers started us Americans thinking. Many of us had to take a second look at our life.

On October 7, 2002, I was headed to work as usual. I made a right turn on a street that had been having a lot of maintenance being done. The right rear tire on my 1988 Mazda sheared off of the spindle causing me to be riding on 3 wheels for a short time before landing safely. God took care of me and prevented me from flipping over. He also made sure I made it safely to work with minimal emotional upset.

Each day I now do face my mortality but differently. I thank God for the peace and serenity He has given me. He has shown me in many ways He is a great God. He has blessed me many times over especially with my life. I now live for Him totally.

I believe Jesus as man, faced His mortality a few times before going to His death on the cross. The 1st time was when Satan asked Jesus to throw Himself from the temple to be saved by His angels. He also faced His mortality the garden when He prayed and faced the vision of the death He would experience for our sins that we would be saved. The last time was finally on the cross when He yelled out; "Father, why has Thou forsaken me?"

The apostle Stephen faced his mortality when being accused of blasphemy. Before he was stoned to death by Saul and others he had a vision from heaven. He shared what he saw in front of his accusers. He testified about the Lord Jesus Christ and God. He repeated the same words that Jesus used when he died, "Forgive them for they know not what they do!"

The apostle Paul throughout his ministry faced his mortality. This happened each time he went out to preach. Once he was stoned and left for dead. Another time he almost drowned. The thing is he was able to survive through his prayers and belief that Jesus is our salvation. There are many stories like this in the Bible.

During this past year I was blessed by being able to experience the death of one of my beloved sisters in Christ. Mary and I would spend hours praying and discussing various parts of the Bible. She lived her life always for her family and others without making any judgments or having prejudices.

As a Licensed Vocational Nurse she would perform her job as a non-complaining servant even though she would be discriminated against. She would pray with her brothers and sisters who were ill. She planted many seeds during this process. In her last days she still wanted to do for others before doing for herself. She faced her final fate or mortality willingly as Jesus did in the end. I believe this is why God allowed Mary not to have very much suffering when she died of Cancer on July 26, 2002.

Until this day I continue to view her as what a caring, loving, and true example of what a Christian should be. If I even had the strength and belief the size of a mustard seed as she had, I would feel I am blessed. I try to now guide my life after this beautiful sister.

In November of 2003 I witnessed the loss of another friend. Her name was Jacquelyn and she passed away in my home while I was at work. She was a new believer that accepted Christ after an anger toward God for over 12-years. Even in her child-like ways she had a sweat outlook on life and became an example for me to follow.

Like I have said, to many of us take our mortality for granted. We think that we can do unbelievable things that are beyond our means without any repercussion. We also think we can do them by ourselves. Guess what? We are very wrong in every aspect. We are not perfect. We make to many mistakes in our life. We need others to help us. Especially God.

Part 2

I Cry From Within.
By: PJ (Author 2009)

Introduction

The story you are about to read is true and not one of fiction. It will discuss how an individual has learned to survive and live with depression and other problems their whole life. You will observe internalized tears, actual heartbreak, growth and strength through the Holy Spirit.

All of us have deal with ups and downs every day. From experience we have learned to adapt and make choices. The reality is not all of the choices that we make are sound or without consequences. Many of us are afraid to take a risk for fear of being hurt or hurting others. I hope that you enjoy what you read.

Since writing this book I have several short stories, newsletters, and an autobiography. This book takes a slightly different twist since it is not written in the "first person." I hope that you enjoy what you read.

By: PJ (Author 2009)

Disclaimer

The various journeys you are about to embark on were taken from actual and true events. The names were changed to prevent hardships or conflicts. Since the writing of this part some of the real characters have since passed on and went to be with the Lord.

By: PJ (Author 2009)

Dedication

This book is being dedicated to those individuals who are always there when you need them. These are true friends who will be there whether it is thick or thin. It also is dedicated especially to God who gives personal strength through the Holy Spirit.

We all are remembered and loved.

By: PJ (Author 2009)

Choices Without Love

During most of his life Jon has suffered from not truly being loved. While growing up his family never was a close knit one. Al (his dad), always abused his mom Anne. When he was done there he would take out his aggression on his seven children. This abuse happened when he was drunk, but sometimes it didn't matter if he drank or not.

When he came home from work it was just best to get out of his way unless you want to be his next target. Of course this was not very hard to do since we always have lived in large houses in Milwaukee, Wisconsin.

Al initially was in the Marines. When Jon was born Al denied that Jon was his true son. In fact, he even thought that Anne was cheating on him. This is part of the reason that he waited so long to marry her. Jon almost grew up being a bastard child.

When Al was discharged from the Marine Corps he worked initially in the local foundry. The work was very hard and grueling, but he was able to manage because physically he was capable of working hard. If anything this was one of his assets.

After work Al would spend a good part of his money by going out drinking with the guys he worked with. Some nights after work, Al would be out all night and have to be back to work early the next day. This pattern and behavior would happen almost 5 days a week. There were even days when he received very little sleep. He also never would spend any quality time with his family.

Being the eldest of seven children Jon would pay close attention to what most of the arguments in our family were about. He knew that when he had his own family that he would never work as hard as his dad, or be abusive. Instead of working hard he would learn to work smart. Little did Jon know that the anger, hatred, and contempt Al showed was a curse and would haunt him the rest of his life?

At the age of eleven Jon started drinking alcohol, smoking pot, and cigarettes just to cope. Due to his maturity and height Jon was able to go into bars and get served. There were very few times that he ever was carded because he did look the part and carried himself several years older than his actual years.

As a teenager Jon would find ways to get alcohol. He would steal from others and even make up excuses just for a drink. This is why by the age of fifteen he became an alcoholic. It wasn't until he went into the military that he became a heavy-duty drug addict and a hard-core alcoholic.

While in the military, Jon discovered that there was a history of drug abuse, alcoholism, and mental illness in his family. He also knew he was different, confused, and possibly even gay. Due to this new knowledge, Jon would try to escape from reality by self-medication. This is why he tried to follow a similar path to the one that his dad and mom had followed when they were in their early twenties.

During those first years that Jon spent in the military he would drink, smoke marijuana, popped speed and dropped acid pills a lot. The only drugs Jon didn't try were cocaine or heroin. He stayed high as much as possible just too get through each day. He would even steal from his peers just to fund these habits.

Eventually all of this partying did catch up with him. When he was becoming a father of a beautiful baby girl, he was stoned out of his mind. After finding out about the birth of Tory he was given an ultimatum from her mother Bea. He was told, "If I don't get off of the drugs that I was taking, you will not see your child." Since Jon took this threat to heart, he did clean up his act.

Jon went through the initial withdrawals from the alcohol and drug mix. He learned how to manage his other problems through assertive training and talk therapy. Since he was doing better he still had not resolved all of his other problems. Eventually after about three months he was completely clean and was able to see his daughter for the first time.

Once completely off of the drugs and alcohol Jon's performance as a soldier improved immensely. This was demonstrated by the rapid promotions he received in less than one year. Jon even became an expert in his field and a general recognized his potential.

While Jon was improving with his military career, Bea was cheating on him and being a hypocrite. She was not living what she preached to when Tory was born. Instead of "Waking the walk" and "Talking the talk," she went out drinking, doing drugs, and whoring around while Jon was in the field on maneuvers. Of course when all of these behaviors happened Jon would get into trouble. These behaviors also continued for about five years before Jon realized that there was no true love there in the relationship anymore. Eventually while stationed in Germany Jon was informed on his birthday that Bea wanted to divorce him. This made Jon very upset and psychotic because he felt that this bomb could have been dropped prior to his birthday or at an earlier time. To him it would have been easier to just not have Bea and Tory to join him in Germany. He knew that there would have been fewer problems. Eventually Jon and Bea had to separate because he almost killed her with his bare hands.

When the separation initially occurred, Jon transported Tory back to Wisconsin so she could be raised by his parents. In order to do so, he had to get a passport for Tee. Getting a passport meant making a drive to Heidelberg, Germany. The drive took about eight straight driving hours and obtaining the passport went well. Shortly after this trip Tory was on her way back to the United States.

After Jon returned to Germany he went back to the partying the way he was doing before he cleaned up. Jon no longer cared what would happen to him. He even took the risk of sleeping around. During these relationships there was no love, just lust. As you can see here poor choices were made and they were without love.

Once Jon was discharged from the military, He tried to raise Tory (his daughter) on his own. He had a lot of problems doing so because he could barely care for himself. These behaviors lead Jon to placing Tory with the state for her protection.

Complete Denial

Shortly after placing Tory with Jon's parents he became confused messed up from the drugs and alcohol that he had been using for all of those years. There was a lot more psychosis, paranoia, abuse, immaturity, and lust. These are things that no child should see or be a part of as they are growing up.

Even though Jon had a good job he still found that he still suffered from gender dysphoria (an identity disorder). He also was confused, and treating himself for major depression with suicidal ideation tendencies with the drugs and alcohol. These were poor choices because Jon never truly dealt with the real problems at hand or in his life.

Many of these behaviors were driven by a very angry individual. This anger was so out of control to the point Jon would sabotage his job performances and life not knowing he was doing so. When Jon finally discovered what was happening, he was in denial and it was too hard for him to believe.

Jon always thought of himself as being highly intelligent, carefree, and an individual without any problems. Little did he realize that he was very wrong and had set himself up for a rude awakening. The reality is Jon had no clue and was in denial about how he presented himself to others. He was so self-centered that he thought he was always right and would strive toward total perfection. This is why just living his life has been harder to do than it ever had to be. Jon needed to really look at himself and grow up. Per say, he had to go back to his roots and discover what reality truly was.

When Jon was not in a relationship with women he would turn to men or himself again. He felt that all he was looking for is for someone to care for and love him even if the relationship was different or out of the norm. Jon always was in fights and never did have many friends. He was lost into himself.

While living an alternative lifestyle Jon tried to discover who he was as a person. Of course this meant traveling around the United States, Canada, and Europe. Some of the traveling he did was when he was in the military. The traveling was done either by airplane, driving or hitchhiking.

Most of the time while on the road he learned that he was a survivor no matter what. Finally Jon arrived in Orange County California in the spring of 1978.

During the first few weeks in Orange County Jon lived in the streets. This only happened because he didn't know better and was too proud to seek out help from others. Jon was still in denial about having any emotional or mental problems. This denial contributed to his decision-making and the poor choices that he continued to make. Jon finally did find a room to rent within a week.

The room Jon rented was several miles from where he worked selling shoes. He started off by walking the distance to work. After he received his first check he learned to ride the bus system. By the end of the first month Jon was resourceful and purchased a bicycle and used it mainly for work.

During the time that he was renting a room Jon continued to

party by going to bars and drinking. He enjoyed the company of just having others around him. The more the better and this would help him craw further into his own self-centered shell.

After renting for two months he met a woman six years older that he was and started to hang out with her. In fact, Jon and Kat became inseparateable and were usually seen together. Both loved to party and were searching for something or someone.

Kate was six years older that Jon and was a hooker with the maturity level of a 5-year old. To Jon this didn't matter. He just thought that Kat was his soul mate. Kate felt the same way toward him but really was going to use Jon.

Shortly after Jon purchased a 1963 Ford Galaxy 500, he decided that he had enough with living in California. This is when he decided to take off and return home to Wisconsin. When Kate heard about the trip she became excited and decided to come along for the ride mainly because she wanted to try something new.

This old vehicle was a 1963 Ford Galaxy 500 and it did well for about half of the trip. About a 24-hours went by when the front axle broke. This was shortly after picking up a couple of hitchhikers and partying with them.

When this axle broke Jon did not have enough money to get the damage fixed, so he decided to hitchhike himself. He figured that he could make better time traveling alone. Little did he know that this original plan was not going to happen. Kate became his traveling companion.

Facing a Violent Reality

While on the road hitch-hiking Jon had to face the reality that he might not make it back home to Wisconsin alive. The reason is because it was in the middle of winter and very cold. To add fire of the problem he now had an unwanted traveling companion that knew almost nothing about being on the road in the cold weather. Being the man of this unusual couple meant that Jon had to take care of himself and another person. He was not even sure that he could do either.

As Jon and Kate continued to hitchhike toward Wisconsin, they were picked up by a group of truck drivers. Initially these truckers fed Jon and Kate and put them up in a hotel room for several days. The reality was Kate was paying for these amenities by providing prostitution services on the side. Finally after being on the road for about a week Jon and Kate made it to Milwaukee, Wisconsin.

Once they arrived Jon contacted a family member and he helped them out for one night. Shortly after contact was made, Jon and Kate found a room above a bar and this family paid the bill for one week.

Several days after getting settled into the new room Kate started to have epileptic seizures. Jon was not familiar with seizures and found out that Kate had epilepsy and stopped taking her medication. Any little thing as the word, "Boo" would cause a seizure to happen. Of course these seizures freaked Jon out but after about two weeks he learned how to work with them. He also learned about some of the signs that he was observing could possibly give him a sign that a seizure might occur.

While living in this room above a bar Jon realized that he had already been through a lot with the hitchhiking, responsibility, and the seizures his companion was having. This is when he lost it and decided that he should seek out psychological help.

Since he was a Viet Nam era veteran, he felt that he could get free assistance with the Veterans Administration hospital there in Milwaukee, Wisconsin. The reality is all that he really needed was rest and time away from Kate. Of course this was a manipulation ploy. He still was in denial about what was truly bothering him. This is why the help that he sought was not effective.

Shortly after the hospital stay Jon found a position as a taxicab driver. This was a job that he had in the past and became pretty good at. With this position he also received veteran benefits from the Social Security office. The reason is because he needed to be retrained since all he knew was the retail business.

The money Jon received with the money Kate received from being disabled assisted them in moving from the one room into a one-bedroom apartment. They were also able to obtain new furniture.

After living in the new place for about a month the relationship between Kate and Jon started to become violent. They were always fighting either verbally or physically. Usually Kate would be on the receiving end and would sometimes get hurt.

During these fights Jon realized that Kate was suffering from multiple personalities. He counted at least ten that he was aware of. Even with the little medical background he had from the military he never dealt with an individual or situation like this.

In order to deal with these problems he had to find a personality within himself that could communicate with those that Kate presented. Several months went by before Jon was able piece what had happened to Kate in the past.

Kate married at the age of fifteen. During the marriage she and her husband became involved in the drug scene. Besides doing various types of drugs Kate would get beat up by this husband. He would bash her head into walls, concrete, and even hit her across her stomach when she was pregnant with one of her boys. The residual of this abuse is she became an epileptic and she left the relationship for her own protection. Shortly after leaving this relationship she resorted back to her drugs and prostitution just to survive. This all went on for many years. Her parents even gave up on her at times because she became uncontrollable and was in and out of mental institutions. Kate created multiple personalities to deal with new situations and environments. Eventually these personalities completely took over her life and she forgot who she really was. The whole process of piecing this entire story together took about 8-months of one-to-one communication and a lot of violence.

Once Jon had the story, he shared what he knew with Kate. When it looked like Kate discovered and accepted what happened she started to become one single person again. The sad part is as improvement happened with Kate, the violence did not stop. This is when Jon decided it was getting close to the time for them to return to California.

Prior to moving back to California Jon did work as a security guard and put aside some money towards the trip. Around December 1978 Kate and Jon were on the road again. This time they left Wisconsin in a 1968 Catalina sedan.

While on the road this time they did not pick up any hitchhikers. Jon also decided that by the time they hit Colorado they were running out of money. This is when he sold the automobile and bought bus tickets to Santa Ana, California.

The bus trip to another couple of days. During that time we did not starve and we ended up being a lot warmer even though it was the beginning of winter.

Once in Santa Ana, we took a taxi to Kate's parent's home. This time they were more accepting. They put us up in a room in their place and fed us. Jon and Kate shared the road ventures with them and stayed up most of the night.

Kate and Jon lived together and eventually married. The relationship continued to be a violent one. Eventually Jon did seek help again and had several nervous breakdowns. He ended up on medications for many years. Kate was getting better in many ways but did try to commit suicide at least 7-10 more times prior to their separation. Finally about 1-year after being separated and divorced Kate did succeed at suicide. She took 76 Fiorecets, washed them down with alcohol, and had a final epileptic seizure. Her final autopsy read death by aspiration pneumonia secondary to a drug and alcohol overdose.

The signs were there with a final note to her mom and dad. It read:

"I want to thank you for everything that you have done

for me. I also want you to thank Jon for the downers in my life."

Kate

Baby Steps

As everyone knows our parents have made the choice to be with each other. These choices are made by what they believe is love, trickery, arrangements, or planned relationships. There might even be manipulation and cheating on the sly. No matter what the case may be, some of these marriages do not always work out. Others end up lasting a lifetime and being an abusive relationship. Finally there are those who believe that their relationships are blessed by God.

Children are not always planned. Some children are even born way before they are planned or by accident. When this occurs there is always something lost in the relationship. The loss is love and caring.

Our love is usually concentrated more toward the child and not our significant partner. An exception, to this premise is when there is some type of balance between both parents and children. Of course cases like this are few and far between.

When all love is lost then some major choices are needed. Here the choice is to either leave or remain together. Most parents make this decision for the benefit of their children. Some choose to stay together through "thick and thin" no matter what even if they are being abused.

When we are born and are children our parents are tasked with making decisions for us. The reason for this is because at a young age we do not know the difference between right and wrong. We just are too young to make decisions for ourselves.

We remain in this dependent mode until we grow old enough to make some decisions for ourselves.

As a typical child one can start making decisions like this between the ages of 3-5 years of age. I believe this was the time Jon started making some choices for himself. You might think how can this be?

The death of Kate devastated Jon. He knew that eventually it was going to happen but didn't know when and how. He knew for a long time that there was no real love in the relationship for a long time. He also knew that her death would happen by accident because Kate "Cried wolf" and made so many suicide attempts in the past. This is why he left for his own survival.

Jon became really confused and during this time he needed love or at least another person to talk too. This is why he jumped into another relationship. This time it was with a nurse that he worked with.

The nurse had three children and was still married. Jon even moved in but that ended up being a very poor choice. He didn't allow himself to heal. This is why he had to learn how to live on his own all over again.

He tried to seek help from his mom, but because of the abuse she received from his dad she would not help. She was just holding her own to survive the abuse she was receiving. Even with Jon's brother and sister living close by, he still felt all alone and not loved.

Love in Wrong Places (a look at the past)

When Jon was younger he would hide out in his parent's room. He would put on his mom's clothes and look through his dad's pornography books and magazines. While doing so he would play dress-up, and masturbate.

He fantasized that he was getting some type of love from these inanimate objects even if it was only self-sexual gratification. He thought nothing about all of this at the time but these behaviors was the start of knowing that he was different. Little did he know that these behaviors would continue on throughout the rest of his life.

Throughout his teen years he was always fighting. He buried his confusion in alcohol and drugs. His parents were never there to talk to about these problems so he kept them bottled up inside. Eventually he knew that he was going to explode because keeping everything inside is not healthy.

As a means of survival he chose to keep my mouth shut. He did not want to be a part of my dad's and mom's battles as his brothers and sister were.

This was denial about the dysfunctional family that he lived in. He made the poor choice to keeping things to himself.

One of the things that he found that worked was to keep busy. He did so by getting his first job as a paperboy. This gave him the chance to be away from the house after school while making his own money.

He had the largest route in the newspaper station. He also made sure that his folks did not know how much money he made. If they knew they would ask me for money. He also knew they wanted it for booze. He was not going to give in to them because he had my own habits to supply.

Since Jon was making his own money, his folks decided that he should buy his own clothes. They even allowed him to go out more. Of course this was enabling him, which eventually would get me in trouble. Eventually Jon went into the military.

When Jon didn't get his own way he jumped back into his old habits. He let Satan take over his life and lost in the process. He had no one blame but myself. It took at least 3 more nervous breakdowns, therapy, and medication, to finally find the answer. This was again without love (or so I thought).

Accepting Change

Today after a lot of hurt, drugs, alcohol, and without love Jon finally found out who he really was. He found out that in order to love someone and receive love, He had to first learn to like and love himself. He needed to now take care of himself without being prideful. Jon also had to learn to forgive and stop judging others and myself. If he didn't do so he would be stuck on the same path he started at and never gets any better.

Even have suffered through at least 5-6 nervous breakdowns during the past 30 plus years there was hope.

Jon Today

Jon has sought out help. After over 40 years of therapy and being on psychotropic medication Jon is doing better. He still does have times when he looses his temper and suffers from frequent mood swings. He is capable of holding down at least one job, but even this is difficult for him. As most alcoholics and drug addicts he has flash backs and black outs. There are many times when he becomes forgetful and overwhelmed.

Jon still does regress back to those old habits that he had in the past. Most days though he has been taking each day at a time.

Part 3

Stages
Someone who has been suffering from
mental illness all of their life
By: PJ (Author 2009)

Dedication

To those of use who have been suffering a mental illness all of
our lives we can survive if we continue to take our medication.
Many of use speak up but no one hears us because we are wired
differently than those who are considered normal. Our voices need
to be heard.

By: PJ (Author 2009)

Disclaimer

Some of the names mentioned in this book have been changed so that there will be no hard feelings. Similarities to actual events may be incidental even though some of the stories discussed may be true.

By: PJ (Author 2009)

Boys will be boys

Joe was born around Christmas time in 1953. He was only six pounds and ten ounces at birth and popped out of his moms' womb two weeks early. Being premature Joe still seemed fairly healthy. His only major problem was he was small but his weight was okay since he was born early.

Joe was the first child of Bertha and Ralph. Of course Ralph could not believe that Joe was his because of the timing of the birth. This is why at first he didn't want to marry Bertha. Instead he just wanted to continue to party with his friends.

As Joe was growing up, he suffered from many allergies. He was allergic to almost everything. These allergies made it difficult for Bertha because she was taking Joe to the hospital all of the time. What complicated matters, is Ralph was being a jerk and would not help Bertha watch or care for Joe. Joe missed the love that he could have had from his dad. He ended up being a Mamas' boy since his mom was the only one that paid any attention to him.

Several years went by when Bertha had another child. This new baby was another boy. His name w as time and he was carried full term.

Initially Tim was pretty sick and had several bouts of Scarlet Fever. There were times when he almost died due to respiratory distress and fevers above 106 degrees. Tim was a fighter so he survived this illness and brushes with death.

Shortly after Tim was born, Joe became jealous. He saw that Tim was getting all of moms' attention. He was starving for attention of his own and even felt that he was being neglected and not loved any more. This is when he would "act up" or "act out." When Joe didn't get his way, he would have tantrums. With these tantrums, he would make messes.

Joe couldn't talk yet so his mom had a problem handling and managing him. If Joe received all of the attention then Tim would be neglected or vise-versa. Bertha had her hands full with these two little boys. By the time Tim was one years old Bertha finally was able to manage the boys.

Joe continued to have a problem walking. He kept running into windows and doors. This happened because he couldn't see them or determine the ending from one to the other. He was basically blind because his eyes would be crossed most of the time. Joe also was a very slow learner.

Tim was walking and running without any problems by eighteen months. By the age of two years old, he was able to make words out for himself and started speaking in complete sentences. In fact, he completely passed Joe up in all of these areas.

Having Tim pass him up was not an easy adjustment for Joe. The reason is Joe thought that he should always be better that his brother especially since he was about two years older than Tim. Of course by not being able to keep up with Tim and not having a loving dad that cared made Joe depressed and left other emotional with psychological scars.

Bertha did not think much about the problems that Joe was

experiencing. All that she knew is Joe was slower than Tim. She thought that through time eventually Joe would catch up and pass Tim. She saw that this is what happened in her family so why not now with these two boys.

By the time, that Joe was at the age of five, Bertha showed some real concern. The main reason is because Joe was still a lot slower than Tim. As she took a closer look at the problem, she consulted her family doctor. The doctor recommended that Joe have surgery to correct his eye problem. He thought that if the eyes were corrected Joe would eventually catch up and even pass his brother up. Bertha agreed and Joe was scheduled for surgery.

Around the time that Joe was to have his eye surgery, Joe and Tim had to go to the hospital. They both were scheduled to have their tonsils and adenoids out. Of course, Bertha and Ralph were not ready for two children being in the hospital at the same time. This is when they started to argue over money.

All of these surgeries went. After only two weeks, Tim was released from the hospital. A week later Joe joined him at home.

Having the boys, back at home ended up causing Bertha a lot of work again. She

had to try to keep them from getting so rowed up and from breaking their internal sutures. This was hard to do because Joe and Tim were always picking on each other.

About a month after being out of the hospital, everything was back to normal. Joe was no longer running into things.

Around Christmas time, Bertha would dress Joe and Tim in similar clothing. She thought that since the boys were about the same size that it would be cute to dress them like twins.

Joe did not take to the twin thing well. It just made him

feel inferior to his brother, which added to his previous scarring. He felt very out of place and didn't think that he fit in with this family.

As both Joe and Tim started school Joe saw that he was behind in his classes. He could not print his name, count, spell, or read. These handicaps caused Joe to be placed behind a year. Tom was doing all of these even before he started school so he was placed ahead of his peers.

Being slow like this made Joe depressed even more. He didn't know why he was dumper than his younger brother. He thought that he should be smarter than Tim since he was two years older. This is where most of the competition for love really affected Joe the most.

During the grade school years, Joe and Tim would always compete with each other. If Joe played baseball, basketball, or football, Tim could do these faster and better. This was the same way in school because Tim would always be reading something new. Joe struggled through his courses and would barely pass them while Tim would breeze through with very little or no effort.

Tim being ahead of Joe was not always a good thing. Tim would also think that he was better than his parents Bertha and Ralph. This is why he would argue with them or tell them off. Behavior like this kept time in trouble with his parents. He was always grounded and had to stay at home most of the time.

Joe would keep everything bottled up inside. Doing so made him very shy but he was given more freedom to do things that he liked to do. He was able to hide things more, and do things on the sly without getting caught. Instead of taking advantage of these privileges, Joe would mainly keep to himself and mope around the house.

As Joe entered into his teenage years he to was never home. He was either working, doing something for school or the Irving Boy's Club, or out with his peers somewhere. As long as he kept his curfew, or called, he could stay out most of the time until early morning.

With Tim being so athletic, he was involved in many sports events at school. He was a very good runner and did well with basketball, and football. As long as he stayed out of trouble and kept up with his grades, he could participate in all of these sports.

During Junior and Senior High, Joe and Tim seemed as opposites instead of twins. Tim was the typical Jock and bookworm. He never dated. Joe was in various gangs and was considered "the gangster" or "black sheep" of the family. He is the one that could care less about sports, dated many girls, drank alcohol, stole, and was always in a fight even if he did loose these fights most of the time. The unique thing though about he was an artist.

Being an artist was only one of the ways that Joe could release his anxieties. The drinking and getting high was his main escape from reality. He would drown his depression away in beer or hard liquor.

Becoming a Man

By the time, Joe and Tim were close to the end of high school they both decided that they wanted to get away from Bertha and Ralph. Joe started to do so by first running away. When he found out that running from his family and problems wasn't working for him he went into the military.

Tim chose to continue his argumentative behaviors. In fact, these behaviors became so out of control that Ralph placed him into a detention home. That is where he stayed until he became eighteen years old.

The military was a shocking experience for Joe. He didn't know that he was going to be abused by the drill sergeants. He also had to do a lot of work to just keep up. The work he did was similar to the experiences that he had while growing up.

To become what the military believed was a man he had to learn and endure the training that he was receiving. This training consisted of running, hand-to-hand combat, carrying heavy loads on your back, firing weapons, and driving. All of this training would take place in a matter of eight weeks.

At first, Joe felt overwhelmed by the amount of effort that he had to put in. He even thought about dropping out before he was half through with the training. His superiors convinced Joe that he was doing well so he stuck it out until his training was completed.

Even through the training, Joe was not able to discuss how he was feeling. He was homesick and missed the little bit of love he received from his mom Bertha. He never received guidance or a caring word from his dad Ralph.

Joes' way of coping was first to bury his feelings and emotions. Of course doing so was nothing new for him because he had been doing so for so many years. When everything got too much for him to handle he went back to his old ways of first drinking alcohol. From here he moved from marijuana and the to speed or acid.

During the 1970's, drugs were very available. Many soldiers ended up getting hooked or messed up from these drugs especially since the ending of the Viet Nam war was near. Since Joe was already a follower, he fit right in.

Tim finally was released from the detention home when he turned eighteen. After being released, he did not return home to Bertha and Ralph. Instead, he also went into the military but instead of staying in, he decided to get out after only ninety days. He felt that he was against firing weapons and around this time, he started to have symptoms of multiple sclerosis.

Before being discharged from the military, Tim left without authorization. This is when he ended first started traveling. He finally ended up on the hippie side of town and join the drug and alcohol circuit until he was finally caught and discharged from the military with a medical honorable discharge.

Party Time and Trouble

As I already mentioned at first being in the military was tough for Joe. His way of adjusting was to become a follower as he had been doing most of his adolescent years. This way he would be in less fights. The sad thing is Joe still was not mature enough to not be influenced by the bad seeds of the company that he was assigned too.

For the first couple of weeks everyone was limited to the base. Shortly after that period, there were many weekends. During those times most of the guys in the company would go into Salinas, California to score, beer, drugs, and women. This means they would be gone throughout most of the weekend. Of course until everyone became comfortable with the area they went to the Enlisted Men's Club which was located right on the beach of the Pacific Ocean.

Due to Joes' past, he held his own with the drinking of alcohol and smoking of marijuana. He still was somewhat shy, so he bottled a lot up inside. To him partying was in a sense his release even if the escape from reality was only temporarily.

Joe barely made it through Basic Training. Part of the reason is because of his inability to interact well with his peers. The other reason is because he was always sick. Sometimes I feel that the

Commanding Officer and Non-commissioned Officers just felt sorry for him and passed him because they needed bodies.

During his first leave before going to Fort Carson, Colorado Joe went for a thirty day, leave. While on this leave he finally went to a Homecoming Dance with Pat (a girl he felt he loved). At that dance, both Pat and he got pretty drunk and stayed out almost all night. The day before returning to Fort Carson he purchased a hallucinogenic called "blotter acid" and dropped the whole thing while staying in his parent's home.

That night Joe did not have a very good trip from the acid. He had many complete body aches and hallucinations. He even became paranoid because he thought he would get caught and couldn't explain what was going on. Later Joe found out that all of these were caused by the strict-nine in the acid. The following day Joe was headed to Fort Carson in his new 1972 Gremlin.

The trip to Fort Carson, Colorado only took Joe twenty-four house. It only took this amount of time because he drove between ninety-five and one hundred miles per hour through most of the states. Of course driving at these speeds was illegal, but Joe was so pumped up on coffee and speed that he didn't care.

Once Joe reported in at Fort Carson he was told to take his time. Hearing that good news, Joe made friends with some new people from other cities. He befriended them and found out that since he had his own ride that they would keep him high or drunk.

The total processing in time took Joe a month. During that time, he only had to attend courses for half days. That would mean by early evening he was ready for partying and going into Colorado Springs.

For that whole month, there were very few days that Joe was wasted from drugs or drunk from all of the beer and hard drinks that he drank. Even being with these people he still felt alone and as if he didn't quite fit in. He also knew that he was being used because of the wheels that he had.

By the time that Joe arrived to Advanced Individual Training, he was a wreck. Again, he was told to take his time to process into the unit. Of course Joe didn't mind because this gave him the opportunity to get to know his peers in the unit. He especially wanted to learn about those who partied as he did.

Advanced Individual Training was no picnic for Joe. He was bored stiff and at one point was injured by a tank hood dropping on his hand. Joe was not given the opportunity to grow or get promoted. Again, Joe felt like he didn't quite fit in.

During this training, Joe showed his true colors. He would steal and fight when he was high. He also was the unit NARC so no one in the upper command would do anything. Eventually when he would get caught he would continue to try to lie his way out, but Joe was a terrible liar.

Joe did get caught a lot. When he did he usually ended up paying for his mistakes financially. Of course, this wasn't always the case. Again, these were poor choices that Joe made. Finally, Advanced Individual Training was over after a couple of months. This is when Joe started to work with his new engineering unit.

Shortly after being separated from his peers in the tank unit Joe requested to change his duty assignment. He felt that he was not a good candidate for heavy lifting. This is when he requested training to become a MEDIC.

It took a couple of months for the MEDIC request to be

processed. During that time, Joe met a girl from Boulder, Colorado. He even married her before starting his new training.

This marriage was one that was not recommended by his superiors. He didn't care though because he thought that he was doing the right thing at the time.

Shortly into the marriage, Joe had his first nervous breakdown. When that happened he would cry hysterically and curl up into a fetal position. At that time, his wife didn't show compassion and added to how he was feeling by pointing a forty-five pistol at him. Finally, the day to go for new training arrived.

Before Joes' leaving Fort Carson, he sent his new bride to be with his parents until he settled in at Fort Sam Houston, Texas. After being in training for a couple of months, Macy joined him in Texas. When this happened Joe found out that Macy was sleeping around and partying on the own when she was with his parents. Of course Joe didn't want to believe what he was told and thought that his parents were wrong.

Having Macy back with him was tough on Joe. The relationship was very rocky mainly because of lack of money and his loss of trust. They were always arguing about something.

Macy and Joe did party a lot together. If it wasn't drinking, it was smoking marijuana and doing harder drugs as acid, methamphetamines, or speed.. This especially got out of control toward the end of Joes' training. He ended almost failing courses due to being high all of the time.

Joe found out through time that he couldn't tell Macy everything going on with him. This included his bouts with depression, phobias, and anxiety. He felt that doing so might end the marriage before it truly had a chance to work. Getting high made it easier for Joe to not deal with everything at once and was an escape from reality.

By February 1973, Joe finally finished his training. He now was a full pledged MEDIC. This is when Macy and he headed back to Fort Carson, Colorado. The trip to Fort Carson, Colorado took about thirty hours. It only took this long because there were a lot of stops along the way.

Once back at Fort Carson, Joe reported for duty the following day. When he did, he received the news that he was finally promoted up one pay grade. With this promotion, he also was to be assigned to the Fort Carson Hospital on a temporary basis.

When he was working in the emergency room, he did learn more than he could comprehend at the time. This was especially true when he learned how to suture wounds and start intravenous fluids.

Joe felt that he was not catching on well at the hospital. This is when he decided that it might be a good experience to work in the ambulance department. Once there he learned what he could by going out on ambulance runs. There were many circumstances or occasions when he just completely missed making the proper diagnosis. This is when he found out that the training he had been through at Fort Sam Houston was very outdated.

One time Joe was assigned to go out on a long distance ambulance run. When he received the assignment initially, he felt uncomfortably about the whole thing and didn't want to take the run alone. This is when he decided to pick up his wife on the way and have her make the trip with her.

That ambulance run was not as easy as Joe thought it would be. While taking a detour, he had a wreck with a military vehicle and his wife was with him. On the way back from the ambulance run it started to snow hard, the patient started to panic and go bad. This is when Joe decided to drop by Fitzimmens Hospital in Denver, Colorado and stay until the snow subsided and the patient stabilized..

As you can see Joe made some very poor choices. He should not have made any detours or picked up his wife. To top these complications off he had an accident while being on one of these detours. If he would have drove straight to Wyoming to pick up the patient and straight back he would not have been in any trouble in the first place.

Macy, Joe, and the patient stayed in Denver, Colorado for a couple of days at the expense of the Red Cross. Finally, Macy and Joe headed back to Fort Carson, Colorado.

On the way, back Joe dropped Macy off at their rented trailer and headed for the post. Once back at Fort Carson Joe reported in and filled out many reports related to the incident and accident. A couple days later, he was administratively released from his hospital assignment and had to report back to his home Engineering Unit.

Shortly after reporting to the unit, Joe was called into the Battalion Commander's office. Of course, the Company Commander was there with him. They both asked me about the accident. Joe was honest with them and told the truth about the incident. Due to his truthfulness, he did not get locked up. Instead he received a reduction of one rank, several months decrease in pay, and was to be restricted to the base for forty-five days.

Joe accepted responsibility for only two of the punishments.

Joe ended up breaking his forty-five day restriction by becoming absent without leave (AWOL). He did so because he wanted to be with his wife.

More Training and a New Family

Of course, no charges were filed because Joe would be going back to Fort Sam Houston, Texas for more training. This time the training was to become a psychiatric technician. The day for the trip for training came up quicker than expected. Joe took Macy with him right away this time. The trip ended up taking around 24-hours. Once in Texas Macy and Joe found another trailer to rent. After getting settled in Joe reported for his training.

The technician course was significantly harder than the Medic course he took about 7-months earlier. To add to the stress of the course Macy was several months pregnant and was having episodes of false labor. She also was becoming dehydrated and eating or sleeping well. All of these problems and the issues Joe was dealing with caused him to flunk out of the psych tech program.

Joe could not manage Macy's pregnancy. This is why he sent her home to her mom's to have the baby. Of course Macy went willingly because she did not want to loose her baby.

Once Macy was out of the picture, Joe decided to live on the base. He figured it would be easier to save money this way. He also knew that there were many drugs available so he could get back to his partying again. In fact, when Macy had the baby he was high on acid.

A Possible New Start

Shortly after the birth of their first child, Joe was scheduled for another transfer. This time he was to be assigned to Fort Riley, Kansas. By being transferred to this new post gave him an opportunity to get a possible new start.

Joe ended up driving his 1959 Lime Green Ford 150 pick-up truck to Kansas. The day that he left, he was high on acid and marijuana. It took a while to straighten out before really making his trip.

On the way to Fort Riley Joe picked up some hitchhikers. These two hikers kept Joe high. They even shared with some of the driving when they could.

The truck looked good for its age but it started to really break down before even hitting Kansas. First, the brakes went out. Next, the truck started to overheat. Eventually the engine block cracked and the truck could not be driven any further. This happened outside of Wichita, Kansas. When the truck finally did give out Joe started hitchhiking himself.

While hitchhiking, Joe headed to Saint Louis, Missouri. He did so because he wanted to search for his brother who was AWOL from the military. He didn't find Tim mainly because he stayed high on marijuana. The traveling on the road also caught up with him so he received a lot of sleep before hitchhiking back to Fort Riley, Kansas.

This time when he hitchhiked, he remained high either on alcohol or marijuana. One of the drivers that picked him up outside of Kansas City was completely drunk. Even drunk he would be perverted toward Joe. Eventually this perversion was too much for Joe. He asked to be dropped off at the next exit.

His final ride brought him just outside of the Fort Riley, Kansas gate. Joe was drunk, but managed to initially check in to the base.

For the next, few weeks after arriving at Fort Riley Joe again went to classes. When he was not in the routine military classes, he started drug and alcohol rehabilitation. All of these took him about two months.

By the end of 1974, Joe was completely free from drugs and alcohol. Once straightened out Joe started to work harder as a MEDIC. His efforts were recognized and he started to make his rank back. Towards the end of 1974, Marcy and Terri joined Joe.

Macy was very impressed with how much Joe had improved. She, Terri, and Joe were able to spend a couple of weeks together before Joe had to go to Germany on maneuvers with the unit he was assigned too.

While in Germany Joe worked harder than ever to gain his rank back. He made himself available for many extra duties. He learned how to be a good MEDIC. Toward the end of the exercise, Joe was shipped home early. The reason is because had Teri taken away from her due to child abuse and neglect. Apparently, Macy would beat up Teri when Teri cried. She also would leave her alone and was not feeding her or giving her enough fluids.

After some time Joe was able to get Teri, back from the courts. This was at the price of having extensive counseling with follow-up visits from the military and civilian department of social services. These visits continued until Joe was to be transferred back to Fort Carson, Colorado.

During the first part of 1975, Joe was transferred back to Fort Carson. While there, he failed out of the Non-commissioned Officer Academy. The reason for this failure was due to the problems that he was having with Macy. He even sent Macy and Teri to visit her mom in California.

While Macy and Teri were gone, Joe continued to make his ranks. He made his Private First Class and Specialist rank simultaneously. Due to his good performance, he became acting Buck Sergeant. Finally, with the assistance of his peers he also received his Expert Field Medical Badge.

During the end of May, Macy and Teri joined him again at Fort Carson. They didn't get to spend a lot to time together because he was going to do a tour in Germany.

Before leaving for Germany, Joe decided to take a leave. The plan was to visit with his immediate family and take everyone with him.

The visit home did not go well. Joe was willing to leave Macy and Teri. The reason is he no longer loved Macy mainly that she abused his child. In addition, he had offered to pay alimony and child support. Of course Macy did not go for this decision. She wanted to try to work everything out. By the end of the month,

Macy and Teri were shipped back to California. Joe was on his was to Germany for his 1-2 year tour.

Joe hated flying to Germany by himself. The reason is because he had a problem with being by himself and he has a problem with motion sickness. He did make the trip though without any incidents.

Once in Germany Joe decided to continue to work harder at his position. Those who knew Joe thought that he was low key. They didn't know that he would drown his problems in alcohol and drugs. They also didn't know that he had been having all of those problems at.

Joe was in denial. He thought that was better than he was. Eventually this delusion-of-grandeur would catch up with him. When it does, he would end up having another nervous breakdown. Eventually that day happened on his twenty-first birthday in Germany. The incident is when his wife decided to divorce him without leaving Germany.

When the incident happened all that Joe could think of is getting their daughter Terri home and out of the picture. Once this was done, he could deal with Macy one-on-one.

It took a couple of weeks, but Terri finally was safe with Joes' parents. When the first part of the trip was completed, Joe returned to Germany to face Macy.

By this time, Macy had become one of the local whores. She was sleeping around with everyone that she met. By doing so, she ended getting Joe into trouble. Eventually Joe was able to get her removed from Germany.

Shortly after his wife left Germany, Joe started back to his drinking alcohol and getting high again. After doing so for several months, he decided that it was his turn to get out of the military. He was fed up with being in a foreign country away from his daughter. Joe figured that he could use the present situation he was in to get out of the military on a hardship discharge. His ultimate goal was to become a single parent and raise his daughter on his own. This is why Joe worked with his mom to put a case together to make the discharge happen. By mid-1976, Joe received the discharge he was trying for. He was head back home to Milwaukee, Wisconsin.

A Civilian Again

Joe arrived home June 30, 1974. Shortly after arriving home, he was a mess. For a person his age he looked a lot older than his years. The main reason is for the past four plus years he had been abusing himself physically and mentally with drugs and alcohol. He still had not accepted that he had a mental illness problem. For many years, he was confused and his head was messed up from the way that he had treated himself in the past. He was lost most of the time.

From 1974 thru 1986, Joe had many different jobs and relationships. It was not until 1986 that he learned about being the "bread winner" while being the head of a family. He also accepted other responsibilities willingly. These roles he managed to maintain for about 11-years. The thing is at what cost?

During these years, Joe ended up being used and became a victim because again he did not truly deal with his feelings. This is why in 1997 when he lost his family that he had several nervous breakdowns in a row. The healing from this was never recognized until he was placed on medication, living life independently, started receiving psychiatric and psychotherapy. True healing did not start until he completely stopped abusing himself.

Today as Joe is approaching his 60's, he is finding out that he definitely is growing old at a fast pace. There are times when he is always in pain, has fallen, been nauseated, had headaches, and fights off nightmares with episodes of insomnia. Joe even has many fears that he continues to face each day.

Joe requires medication just to make it day-to-day. Every step that he takes and day that he is alive is a blessing. Eventually he may require a caregiver to assist him. The problem is he a loner and would rather have a state of peace all of the time. Of course, this peace is an ideal circumstance or situation.

Part 4

All of My Children
By: PJ (Author 2009)

Dedication

This portion of this book is dedicated to all of the children that have been part of my life. Since being married three times I had a total of seven children and stepchildren. Three stepchildren I completed raised with the help of their significant other, two I partially raised, and one I had not had the opportunity to know or raise. In any case throughout the years I have truly loved all of these children and I am sorry that I especially hurt Tammy Lynn and Joshua. I'm sorry that I never had the pleasure and opportunity to meet you or be part of your life April.

By: PJ (Author 2009)

First Born

Jon met Beebe when he was in the United States Army during the summer of 1972. During that time Jon actually took some days off from his post located at Fort Carson, Colorado.

Jon and his best friend Gary decided that they didn't want to hang around the post for the weekend. Instead they headed for Bolder, Colorado, which was, located west of Denver.

The trip to Bolder was about an hour drive from Fort Carson. Of course since Jon would get motion sick being a passenger, he did the driving. The other reason for Jon driving is because it was his car, which was a 1972 Gremlin.

Finally they arrived at Bolder, Colorado by about 5:00 pm. They went to Gary's house first so that he could pick up some more clothes. Then they headed for the ice skating rink and had a dinner if burgers, French-fries, and cokes.

While at the skating rink they saw a group of girls. Since they loved to out due each other they decided to skate with them with the hopes of hooking up with one of them for the rest of the night.

Jon was usually shy when he was straight or sober, but when he was drunk or high on marijuana, speed, or acid he was more outspoken. He would love to take unnecessary risks. He figured that hooking up with one of the girls would not be very risky.

This is why he jumped right in and asked one of the girls to be his skating partner.

The name of the girl that Jon met was Beebe. She was all but 4 foot and 11 inches tall, had a very slim figure with a weight of about 120 pounds, and was beautiful. Her hair was in a bob cut and auburn and her eyes were brown. Even though she was 17 years old she looked a lot younger. The group that she was with was a state boarding home that was on an outing. Since Beebe was a ward of the state of Colorado, seeing her after encounter at the skating rink would be a challenge.

The evening at the ice-skating rink went well. Beebe and Jon just seemed to click and have a lot in common. Everything went so well that Beebe invited Jon to visit her at the boarding home. Of course this would be at the approval of the caregivers.

A week after there meeting Jon took Beebe up on her invite. He called her and she was busy with her chores so she couldn't talk. When this happened, Jon just drove to Bolder be himself and was able to see her. The problem was Beebe only could visit with Jon for a couple of hours each night. Jon continued to meet with Beebe every weekend until one day Beebe was released into the custody of Jon.

Shortly after being released she and Jon were married. Jon was getting ready to start medical training during that November. He wasn't ready for his new wife to be with him so he sent her to stay with his parents in Wisconsin while he attended school in Texas.

The stay with his parents wasn't working out well for Beebe. This is why by the time that Thanksgiving came around Beebe joined Jon.

Jon was not ready for his new wife joining him. He just was

very immature and still had another problem that he had a problem being honest about. This was closet cross-dressing. This problem was not invisible for long in their marriage because Beebe caught Jon dressed in woman's clothing and wearing makeup. When he was caught, Jon would lie but this lie caught up with him. Beebe would dress up in his military gear and actually go out in public while doing so.

By New Years of 1973 Beebe and Jon met their neighbors that lived just below them. Almost every night when Jon was off of work they would get high, share meals, or play cards. Their favorite card games were Spades, Canasta and Double Canasta.

For New Years they planned a potluck party. There was to be good food, drinking, smoking marijuana, and card games if there was time. Little did Jon and Beebe know that this couple had other plans for the evening?

As the night started out there was a lot of talk and good food. Jake informed us that he was a Satanic Priest and a practicing Satanist. He stated that his common law wife who was only 15 years old was one of his followers.

Toward the end of the night this couple wanted us to swing with them. This is when Jake was to be paired up with Beebe and Jon with his wife. Jon did go through with everything but Beebe didn't. From that moment on Beebe could not trust Jon anymore.

By about the middle of January 1973 Beebe was pregnant. She was to have a girl but everything became complicated. This was especially true when Jon was in another program in Texas. This is why Beebe was sent to live with her mom.

On August 10, 1973 Terra was born. The day that she was born

Jon was high on acid. In fact when he received the call that he was a new dad he barely could believe what he heard. Of course Beebe knew Jon was high when she talked with him. This is why she gave him an ultimatum to either quit the drugs or not ever see his baby girl. Jon chose to quit the drugs but not completely.

In September of that year Jon was transferred to his new duty station. This time it was Fort Riley, Kansas. To keep good to his promise to Beebe he started on a rehabilitation program. During the program he was to meet with a therapist a couple times a week and a psychiatrist once every couple of months.

At the end of September Beebe and Terra joined Jon in Junction City, Kansas. They were only there for a week and Jon had to go overseas to Germany for some war games.

During those games Jon proved that he could be a good soldier. He excelled at his job, but that didn't help his career. His little girl was taken away from his mother and Jon had to be shipped back home immediately. A week after being back home Beebe and Jon received Terra back. They were monitored every couple of months from that point on for 1 year.

By late 1974 Jon was transferred back to Fort Carson, Colorado. This time around he was an acting Buck Sergeant in an Artillery unit. As an added duty he decided to become the Training Non-Commissioned Officer (NCO) for the company. This new position helped him get promoted ahead of his peers.

While Jon was working as the Training NCO he worked with his supervisors and peers especially in the field. There even was a program going on where various medics on the base took a program to become an expert in their field. He studied and learned the material with his peers and succeeded by obtaining his Expert

Field Medical Badge. Shortly after obtaining the award he was finally promoted to a Specialist-Five position.

During the summer of 1975 Jon was to be deployed to Germany. The stay was to be for 2-3 years. Prior to leaving though Jon had a 30-day vacation, which he took with his new family in Wisconsin.

While on this vacation Jon had made a decision. He knew that his marriage to Beebe wasn't working. Trust was lost on both sides. He even told Beebe that if she chose to completely leave him that he would accept her decision and be a responsible individual and provide for her and Terra. Beebe and Terra then were sent back to California so that they could stay with her mom until Jon was settled in Germany.

Another thing that Jon and Beebe talked about is trying to regain custody of her first daughter Andrea. The problem is Beebe didn't know where Andrea was

Initially when Jon arrived into Germany he decided that he was going to make the best of everything until his family joined him. He took his time checking into his new unit and decided to start drinking again. Instead of working as a medic all of the time he decided to be a medic when in the field and a Training NCO for his regular position. Since he was staying in the barracks again he partied with everyone on marijuana. When not smoking or staying in the barracks, he would go to the bars drinking. His favorite drink was Conjac and coke.

Jon didn't care about what he did when he was high or drunk. In fact, when he went to one of the bar's located in the downtown area of Aschafenburg, Germany, the bar tender tried to play a trick on him. Instead of just drinking a coke with a small amount of

Conjac, he poured 3/4ths of the glass with Conjac and 1/4th of the glass with coke and dared Jon to drink it. He informed Jon that if he could drink it that his drinks would be free for the rest of the night. Jon guzzled the drink down in less than a minute.

When Jon downed his drink that fast the bar tender and the owner were very impressed. They kept their word and Jon drank free for the rest of the night. A couple of days later Jon found out that both the bar tender and bar owner was gay. They wanted Jon to frequent their bar and possibly become involved with them. Of course Jon didn't know that they wanted him so he ignored them and never came to that bar again.

By Jon's Birthday, which was in December, Beebe had informed him that she wanted a divorce. Of course Jon panicked and sought out counseling. The counseling didn't help though because by February 1976 the paperwork for divorce was initiated and Jon got Terra out of the picture by getting her back to the states to stay with his parents.

Shortly after Jon had Terra home he decided he would get out of the military and send Beebe home. The whole process for getting an honorable discharge took around 3-4 months. He was out of the army by the end of June 1976.

The divorce was being processed so Beebe and her first daughter Andrea were out of his life. Now he tried to raise Terra first in his parent's home, and then by himself. He found out since he was immature and wanted to party again he couldn't raise Terra. Instead he awarded her to the state until his parents stepped in and decided to raise her with Jon paying support.

One and two make four

Around 7 months after being out of the military Jon ended up in California. He started off living in the street because he was completely broke and had no place else to stay. Fortunately once he arrived in California he was able to obtain a job selling men's shoes. With the money that he made he was able to feed himself and initially start buying clothes. By the end of the week he had saved enough money for a place in a board-n-care home.

While living in a board-n-care home me met a girl by the name of Kate. She was a hooker who had a mental illness. That didn't matter to Jon though because at that time all that he wanted is companionship from the opposite sex.

For the next couple of months Jon and Kate were inseparable. They would go everywhere together including going to bars. This is why shortly after Jon bought a car they left California for a trip to Wisconsin.

The trip to Wisconsin took them about a week. The reason is because their car broke down when they were only half way to their destination. When that happened they decided to hitchhike because they didn't have enough money to complete the trip any other way.

Once in Wisconsin they stayed with some of Jon's family for

1 night. From there they moved into a 1-room apartment. This is when Jon truly was able to get to know Kate.

Apparently Kate had been in an abusive marriage in the past. From that marriage she had 2 boys Paul and Mark. The reason that these boys weren't staying with her is because she was the one who walked out on the family just for survival.

Kate and Jon stayed together for almost 8 years. During those 8 years they were able to visit with Mark and Paul several times. In fact, Paul decided when he was old enough that he was going to stay with his mom Kate and Jon. Of course this relationship again didn't work out and eventually Jon left. Shortly after he left Kate went back to the drug scene and started hooking again. Eventually she ended up committing suicide at the age of 38 years old.

One and four is six

Shortly after his separation from Kate Jon entered into another relationship with one of his co-workers. By this time Jon was a vocational nurse working in the skilled nursing called Western Medical Center-Bartlet. The co-worker was a RN from the previous shift. Her name was Shelly and she was married with 3 children.

Shelly would stay over from 2-4 hours on her shift. The main reason was to finish up her work. The other reason is because she had a crush on Jon and wanted to get to know him better.

He shared with her that he no longer could trust Kate because she was now gone all of the time. He even mentioned that she started drinking and using drugs again which for him was the cause for eventually leaving her.

Shelly had many problems of her own with her husband. She felt that Shawn Senior was verbally abusive to her and expected too much of her especially since she was a registered nurse now.

Apparently she was doing all of the housework and he was not chipping in to help. He never even chipped in to help her raise her 3 children.

There was always chaos in her home with all of the yelling and messes from her kids and husband that needed to be cleaned up. This is why Sheila decided to stay longer at work to avoid the reality of a large family.

After about 3-4 months of working together Shelly moved to the 11-7 shift as an alternate supervisor. When this happened Jon was elated because he would have an ally who was a registered nurse.

When Shelly and Jon worked together they were very competitive. They even shared some of the same ideas in nursing and worked well as a team. The thing is though they would let their relationship flow over on to the job and after work, which if caught both of them would have, been fired. Around 2 months later Jon did leave the skilled nursing facility. He even decided to finally leave Kate.

When that happened, Shelly offered to put him up for a few days in her home. This gave her the opportunity to sleep with Jon when she wanted to do so. Eventually Jon was able to move into a 1-bedroom efficiency apartment.

Jon lived in this apartment by himself for about 3 months before Shelly decided to move in with him. Everything was working out well initially and Shelly was able to meet some of the friends that he made while he was working at his new position in a respiratory-neuro-rehabilitation facility.

Shortly after these 3-months she moved in with Jon without her 3 children Shawn Jr., Mike, and Samantha. They had a lot of quality time together between the times that they worked. They even tried to schedule their hours of work so that they could be together more often. This was tough to do since they were now working at different facilities now.

By summer Shelly started to see her kids more. This was tough on their relationship though because Jon was not use to having a ready-made family. Also having five people in a small 1-bedroom was very cramped.

Initially as Shelly's divorce started she had to pat child support. The reason is she walked away from her family.

The court system worked with her soon to be ex-husband and believed that Shelly was making more money than Shawn Sr. because she was a RN. Shelly was against making these payments and wanted to have her kids with her full time. This is why the court ordered a mediator the assist Shelly and Shawn SR to come to a mutual visitation agreement that they would both be happy with.

The divorce median went on for 3-4 months. Eventually 6 months into the process Shelly's divorce was finalized. When the finalization took place Shelly and Jon rushed to the courthouse and got married. About a month after this quickie marriage the had an actual ceremony at Shelly's mother's home for just family and friends.

Around a year after this marriage Shelly's kids Shawn Jr., Mike, and Samantha became part of the family. Now Jon was responsible for not only himself and Shelly, but these kids too. He of course wasn't ready for this drastic change, but being a responsible person he took on the task. Of course life was no longer going to be easy for him.

Jon ended up taking on other jobs. When he finally realized that he had as much if not more knowledge than Shelly he decided to pursue obtaining his RN. This meant going back to college again.

While in college Shelly assisted Jon with some of his studies. This caused some pressure on the relationship too. Of course eventually Jon did finish his step-up LVN-RN program with a decent grade about 3 years later.

The first time that he took the RN boards, he missed passing the exam by only 5 points. A year later though he passed with high scores. This was with the assistance an advanced pretest study program and reviewing study tapes provided him by the dean of nursing from the college he attended. The same year Jon received his RN license Jake was born.

Once he became a RN he started working as a medical-surgical nurse. From there he progressed to become a telemetry nurse and a year later a critical care nurse.

Of course Jon continued to maintain more than one RN position. He did so because he knew if he didn't he family would starve. Shelly also maintained her RN position sat the same time.

They both worked at this level for almost 8 years when Jon decided he was going to become a reserve officer and go back to college to get his Bachelor's degree in nursing.

Again obtaining this higher position and working too meant that Jon would not be home as much anymore.

Jon finished his Bachelor's degree about 1-½ years after starting the program. He was able to test out on some subjects, which made the program easier for him. The military also paid a large portion of the tuition so the burden on the household was kept down to a minimum. He even continued with his military career as an officer.

Within 8-months after obtaining this degree Shelly decided that he no longer wanted to be married to Jon. Instead of being with Jon she had been seeing someone else for at least 6-months.

When Shelly was confronted about Jon knowing about this new relationship she denied it. Within 15-days after the confrontation divorce paperwork was started on both ends.

When all of the divorce paperwork was started Jon completely lost it. He felt that his world was being pulled from underneath him. Even when the divorce was finalized about 6-months later he still was picking up the pieces.

Synopsis

Since the writing of these short stories many things have happened in Jon's life. He has outlived two of his ex-spouses. One committed suicide at the age of 38 years old. The other died recently of a brain tumor at the age of 55 years old. Jon now has 4 grandchildren.

Even with these grandchildren there still is a lot of strain with his immediate family. The only true person that keeps in touch in a 78 year old mother. She even has her own life to live since loosing her husband a little over a year ago.

There are many families with problems more serious that those you read about in all of these previous pages. The main lesson learned though is that no matter what families need to communicate with each other. It doesn't matter about distance or problems that exist we should always unite especially during time of crisis.

About the Author

P.J. Anderson is an individual who has experienced a lot of situations during her lifetime. She definitely has learned and grown through these. This book is the third of three that she has written. The first was an autobiography called: "THREE STRIKES AND YOU ARE NOT OUT," and a series here, "A WORLD OF ABUSE," "I CRY FROM WITHIN," "STAGES," and  "ALL OF MY CHILDREN." She has developed a Web site that she started 11 years ago in California. It is: http://www.geocities.com/pj_1953/page2 She first started her writing at the age 11 years old. She has received awards and went summer at camp for her story "Fatman and the Boy Blubber" at this age She has written several news letters for a church in California during the summer of 2003 and presently publishes an annual news letter for her family and friends called; "THE TEXAS ALPHA." Ms Anderson has been a registered nurse over 20 years and obtained a Masters degree in Healthcare Administration Nursing in 2009. She also has been working with computers since the late 1970's and holds an Associate's degree in this area.

From 2000-2002 Ms Anderson ran two support groups with the Gay and Lesbian Center of Orange County. One was People Experiencing an Alternative Lifestyle (PEAL) and South Coast Transgender Alliance (SCTA). One group dealt with Transgender issues both male and female. The other dealt with drug and alcohol abuse at various levels. Ms Anderson was born as a male in Milwaukee, Wisconsin and has been living as her true self for the past 11 years. She now resides in the San Antonio, Texas area.